SEPARATIONS

Hospital

By Janine Amos
Illustrated by Gwen Green
Photographs by Angela Hampton

CHERRYTREE BOOKS

A Cherrytree Book

Designed and produced
by A S Publishing

First published 1998
by Cherrytree Press Ltd
a subsidiary of
The Chivers Company Ltd
Windsor Bridge Road
Bath BA2 3AX

British Library Cataloguing in Publication Data
Amos, Janine
    Hospital. - (Separations)
    1.Hospitals - Juvenile literature 2.Hospital patients
    Psychology - Juvenile literature
    I.Title
    362.1'1

ISBN 0 7451 5271 6

Printed and bound in Belgium by
Proost International Book Production

CONTENTS

Dear Steven,

Here I am in hospital waiting for my operation. Mum has gone to get a snack at the cafe, so I thought I'd write you a letter as I promised.

When I got here it felt a bit scary. There are loads of people, everyone's busy. It felt strange to know that I'm going to sleep here. I thought I'd have to put my pyjamas on and get into bed. My nurse is called Sara. She's fun. She told me I could stay in my tracksuit. Then she showed me the green gowns and masks the doctors will wear tomorrow for my operation (just like on TV). She told me exactly what will happen to me. I don't feel so worried now.

I have to have an injection before the operation. I told Sara I really hate jabs. She says they'll put some special cream on my hand so it goes numb. Then I'll only feel a tiny prick. I met the doctor too, she prodded my stomach and told me a Knock Knock joke.

The main thing I'm worried about is that I won't be able to go skiing with you after Christmas. I'm scared to ask in case they say no.

Cheers,

Jake

P.S. There's a boy here called Robert. We're going to have a game of cards before the TV goes on.

Dear Jake,

It sounds like hospital's OK. If you're still there next Saturday, Mum's promised to drive us over to see you. She says Children's Wards don't have special visiting times - so we can stay all day. We'll bring you your favourite chocolate cake. Yum!

Your doctor sounds nice - why don't you ask straight out about skiing? It's better than worrying about it.

You'll have a new video to watch soon. Mum and I posted it to the hospital with your name on.

See you, Steven

WHAT'S THE MATTER?

Emily was in her room. She was building a Lego space station. Emily loved building models. But today the pieces seemed too small and fiddly. Her head ached. A fly buzzed at the window and the sun streamed in. Emily was hot and tired. She needed a drink.

Emily went to the kitchen. Her mum was there, chatting on the telephone. Emily's mum spent ages on the phone – she could even cook at the same time! But today, as soon as Emily came in, she put down the telephone.

"What's the matter?" asked Emily.

"Nothing, dear," said her mum, brightly.

"Something's going on," thought Emily, getting herself some juice.

The next morning Emily woke early. On her way to the bathroom, she passed her brother Dan's bed. He was still fast asleep. Emily tiptoed past. Then she heard voices from her mum and dad's room.

"I haven't said anything yet. We'll tell her nearer the time," her mum was saying. Something about her mum's voice made Emily stop and listen.

"She won't want to go, not our Em. There'll be an awful fuss," replied Emily's dad.

"They're talking about me," thought Emily. "They're sending me away!"

Back in bed, Emily thought about her dad's words. Where wouldn't she want to go? And why were they sending her? Her heart began to thump and she felt a bit sick. Had she done something wrong?

All morning Emily watched her mum. She helped her clean up after breakfast. She helped her wash the car.

When the telephone rang, Emily jumped.

"Claire's mother is on the phone," called Emily's mum. "Would you like to go there for lunch?"

Emily shook her head. She wanted to stay at home.

At teatime, Emily couldn't eat. Her headache was worse and she wanted to cry. It was awful, just waiting for something to happen. She went and sat on her bed.

Just then, Emily's mum came in. "Is something the matter?" she asked. Emily burst into tears. "You're sending me away!" she shouted. "I heard you!"

Emily's mum sat next to her on the bed. She gave Emily a big hug.

"Oh, I'm so sorry, Em," she said. "I didn't mean to worry you."

Emily waited for her mum to carry on. "You have to go into hospital next week. You'll need to stay in for a few days. The doctors will do some checks on you. I'll be staying there with you."

"Who'll look after Dan?" asked Emily.

"Nan's coming," said her mum. "It's all arranged."

"Will you be with me all the time?" asked Emily.

"Yes," replied her mum. "And before then we'll visit the hospital together. You can see the Children's Ward and meet some of the nurses. Would you like that?"

Emily nodded.

At last the day came for Emily to go into hospital. She packed a bag to take with her. She put in two pairs of pyjamas, five books, three comics, some new soap and her old Mickey Monkey.

"I don't mind about hospital," said Emily as she climbed into the car. "The thing I didn't like was not knowing."

"I understand that now," said Emily's mum slowly. "I got it wrong, didn't I?"

"That's OK," said Emily, smiling. "Let's go!"

Dear Auntie Jan,

Thanks for your card. Sorry about my writing - it's hard to write lying down! I've had the operation and I feel quite well, but I can't go home yet. When I first got to hospital I have to stay in bed. When I first got to hospital I was checked by lots of doctors and nurses. They gave me X-rays and took blood tests. I couldn't have any breakfast before the operation. Afterwards, I had lots of tubes in me. I wasn't scared because the nurses told me what they were all for and Mum slept on a camp bed next to me.

I thought it would be boring here but it's OK. The nurses are great and there are lots of other children. A teacher comes round every day with work for me. I still have to do Maths, even in hospital! We have a laugh. Yesterday I even made a cake lying down!

I'll be in here for ages. I bet everyone at school will forget about me. Sammie will get to be Kim's best friend. They're doing a project together and working on it after school.
Please write soon.
            Love, Anya

Dear Anya,

It was great to get your letter. You sound as if you're getting on very well in hospital. I'll be in to see you next week.

Are you a bit worried about what's going on at school while you're away? I remember feeling like that when I was ill and off work. Is there anyone you can talk to about it - the teacher, a nurse or your mum? They might have some ideas for keeping in touch with your friends at school. How about writing to Kim and the others?

I'll see you next week, Anya. If you do any more baking, keep a slice of cake for me!

Love, Auntie Jan

FEELINGS: GOING INTO HOSPITAL

When you first learn you'll have to go into hospital you may feel worried. What will it be like?

■ It's natural to feel concerned about a new situation. If you are feeling nervous, talk about it with a grown-up. Together, try to work out what it is that worries you.

■ Some television programmes about hospitals show frightening scenes of operations with lots of blood or big, beeping machines. Children may remember these scenes whenever they think about hospitals. Don't forget, these scenes have nothing to do with you – and they're not real anyway! Hospital's simply a place for trying to make people better.

■ Some children may not like the thought of being away from home. They worry about sleeping in a strange bed without all their usual things around them.

■ Other children worry about leaving their pets behind. Will they be looked after properly?

INJECTIONS

Lots of people hate the idea of having an injection. If you're really worried, tell your parent and make sure the nurses know. Ask if some anaesthetic cream can be put on before the injection. This will make your skin numb so you won't feel the needle. Ask if you can play a story tape to take your mind off the injection. Don't look at the needle. Yell if you need to – but keep still. Remember, it will only prick for a second.

■ Friendships may seem a worry too. Anya is scared that the girls in her class will forget about her. She worries that her best friend will grow to like someone else more.

■ Sometimes, children wonder what they might be missing out on at school. Will they be able to catch up later?

GETTING READY TO GO IN

If you need to go into hospital, there are some things you can do to prepare yourself.

■ Find out why you are going into hospital and what will be done to you. Ask how long you will be there. If you don't understand everything, keep asking. If your parents have any questions they can check with the hospital staff. Ask your parents if you can visit the hospital before you go in.

■ Share any worries with an adult. One of your parents can stay with you in hospital. If they need to go home at any time, together find someone to be with you in their place.

■ Pack a bag to take with you. You might like to pack (with your name on): your favourite toy; your favourite mug or drinking cup (even a bed-time bottle if you think it would help); writing things, books, small toys, games, videos; a wash bag with soap, toothpaste and a hairbrush; cool day clothes (it's often hot in hospital!); two sets of nightwear.

- If you have a pet, get someone in your family or a friend to look after it. Tell them your pet's likes and dislikes, so that you won't worry while you're away.

- Ask if a school friend can visit you in hospital. They'll keep you in touch with what's going on at school. Ask your teacher what the class will be doing while you're away. There might be some work you would like to do in hospital.

EMERGENCY

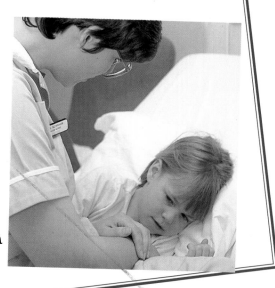

If you're rushed into hospital in an emergency, you won't get time to prepare. There are some things you can do to help yourself cope: Take some deep breaths to help calm yourself. Remember, the nurses, doctors and paramedics are doing their jobs as fast as they can to help you. Ask for someone to explain what's happening. Ask a nurse to hold your hand.

Dear Steven,

Thanks for the video - it's great! I've watched it twice (the second time with Robert, the boy I met here).

I've had my operation and it was OK. I knew what was going on because the doctors and nurses talked to me all the time. Mum was with me and she asked some questions too. They made me go to sleep with an injection, so I didn't feel them doing the operation.

My tummy's a bit sore but the nurse said that will go after a few days. Mum is sleeping here at the hospital in a chair (it pulls out to make a bed). Dad's coming to see me after tea.

I'll be out by Saturday, so Mum says you can come to our house instead of the hospital (you can still bring the yummy cake).

I'm keeping a Hospital Diary of everything that happened while I was in here. I can take it to school and show the class.

See you,

Jake

Hospital Diary

Monday
In Children's Ward. Mum and I met Sara the nurse. I went in the Playroom and met a boy called Robert. Mum filled in a form. Sara checked my height, weight and blood pressure. Ward is busy and noisy. Everyone is friendly. Video next to my bed - great! Won't be able to have breakfast tomorrow before my operation – so I stuffed myself at teatime. Food here is OK.

Tuesday
Woke up early. Sign on my bed: NIL BY MOUTH (it means I can't eat or drink until after the operation). They've just put cream on my hand and it is going numb. So I won't feel the injection.

Photo of me and Robert in the Playroom

Wednesday
My tummy is sore but Sara gives me medicine to make it feel better. Got up and went to see Robert. Don't remember much about yesterday. Worst bit was leaving Mum. She couldn't come into the anaesthetic room. It was a bit scary then, but everyone was chatting and it was OK. Woke up and Mum was here. Had breakfast, lunch, tea and dinner! Watched a new video from Auntie Cath and Steven.

Thursday
Doctor says I'm fine. I can go home on Friday.

Thankyou for looking after me. My stomach is fine now. Skiing is cool. I'm getting quite good. Afterwards we have hot chocolate with cream on top to warm us up.
Happy New Year to you all.
Love from
    Jake Narraway

The Children's Ward
St Michael's Hospital

FEELINGS: IN HOSPITAL

Hospitals are big, busy, noisy places. At first they may seem strange and a bit scary. There are unusual smells, lots of new people, large machines – everything is different from home or school.

■ Because the hospital is new to them and because everyone is so busy, some children feel small and powerless. They feel they can't ask questions. Never be afraid to ask.

■ Don't think your worries are silly. They are not. Some childen worry that their clothes will be taken away, that a strange nurse will bath them, that they'll be somehow different after their operation. These concerns are very real, so tell the nurse or doctor whatever your fears are.

■ For most children, the stay in hospital will be short. Others need to stay longer. Some quickly get used to hospital life, and may worry about leaving.

■ Other children get bored. They find it hard to read or do their schoolwork. They feel cut off from the real world and fed-up with everything.

Operation

If you are to have an operation, you may wonder what will happen. These are the stages:

Before the operation, you won't be able to eat or drink. You'll put on a hospital gown with an open back (you can keep your pants on, if you like).

An hour before the operation, you may have some medicine. It will make you sleepy and your mouth will feel dry.

You may have some cream put on your hand so that the needle for the anaesthetic won't hurt.

Someone will collect you when the operation is due to start. The anaesthetic will make you sleep so that you won't feel a thing. If you want your parent to stay with you, ask when you get to the hospital.

When you first wake up you'll be in the Recovery Room. Then you'll be wheeled back to the ward on a trolley. You might sleep for a long time. A nurse will bring you a drink.

If you have any questions at all about your operation, just ask.

HELPING YOURSELF IN HOSPITAL

There are some things you can do to help yourself settle into hospital. When you get to the ward, sort out some ways to make yourself feel more comfortable.

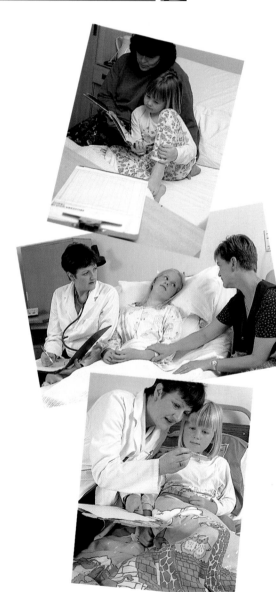

■ As soon as you can, learn your way around. Ask where the toilet is. Find out what the times are for lunch and tea. Is there a playroom? If so, ask when you can visit it.

■ If you're going to have an operation, find out as much as you can about it. Ask a nurse to explain what will happen step-by-step.

■ Remember, all the people around you want to help you get better. Help them to help you by telling them how you feel. Don't keep any fears or worries to yourself. If you are having a long stay in hospital, you can help yourself in other ways too.

■ Keep as busy as you can. Ask your family if they'll bring in some different things to do. Swop games and videos with other children on the ward. Why not learn to do something new – how to braid your hair, play chess or do painting-by-numbers?

■ Use your knowledge of hospital life to help someone else. Chat to the new children on the ward, tell them what goes on and help them to feel more confident. Ask a nurse or the playleader if there's any other way you can help new patients to settle in.

■ Keep in contact with friends at home and at school. Write them letters. Ask your playleader to help you make a tape to send them.

■ Like Jake, keep a Hospital Diary. Write notes about what happens each day of your stay. Then you'll have your own hospital story to look back on when you're home again.

ALEX'S BIRTHDAY

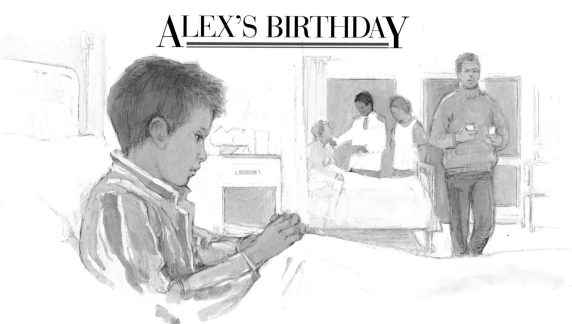

A lex sat straight up in bed. He threw down the comic he'd been reading. He wiggled his toes under the bedclothes and sighed. A nurse went by and smiled at him. Alex didn't smile back.

Alex looked towards the door at the end of the Children's Ward. He could see his dad coming back with drinks from the machine. He closed his eyes and turned his face away.

"I've got some Coke for you, Alex, and hot chocolate for myself. That coffee's awful!" murmured his dad.

Alex didn't want to answer. He felt angry with his dad. He felt angry with everyone. In two days it would be Alex's birthday. He'd be eight years old. And he was in hospital.

The next morning, Alex was woken by someone whistling. A nurse was checking the charts at the end of Alex's bed.

"Hi, I'm Harry!" said the nurse. "Your dad's getting some breakfast in the canteen."

Alex nodded.

"Wow," said Harry. "You're a grouch. Is that leg hurting you?"

"No," said Alex.

Harry pulled up a chair. "Your operation's all set for this afternoon. I'll be around to get you ready. Any questions, I'm your man. I'll tell you exactly what's going on. OK?"

Harry grinned and Alex gave him a wobbly smile.

Harry looked into Alex's face.

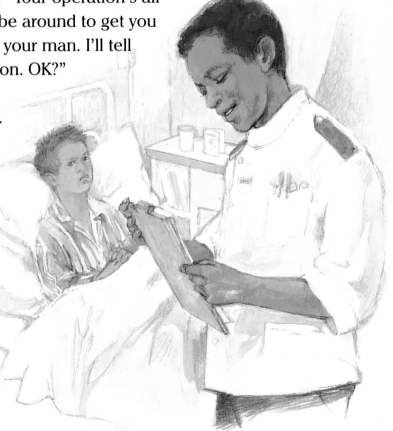

"Wow! I've got it," he said at last. "It's all in your notes. You're the Birthday Boy – and you're stuck here for the Big Day. Is that right?"

"That's right," said Alex, crossly.

"What sort of party were you planning?" asked Harry. "Burger bar? Swimming?"

"The gym," said Alex, quietly, "with pizzas afterwards."

"Mmm," replied Harry, shaking his head. "There's no way you're doing any bouncing tomorrow, not with that leg."

"I know that!" snapped Alex. "I'm trapped in this stupid bed!" He thumped the mattress hard.

"Hey!" said Harry, gently. "Life doesn't stop just because you're in hospital, you know. A birthday's a birthday – right?"

Alex shrugged. "What do you mean?"

"Wait and see!" grinned Harry.

That afternoon, Harry came back again. He got Alex ready for the operation on his leg. Harry explained everything that was going on.

Soon Alex was on a trolley, rolling towards the operating theatre. His dad squeezed his hand as they went along. All the time, Alex could hear Harry's friendly whistling in the background. It made things seem easier, somehow.

Later, Alex remembered someone calling his name. When he woke up properly, he was back in bed. It was night-time. His dad was sitting next to him, snoring in the chair.

Alex drifted back off to sleep.

Alex spent the morning opening birthday cards and presents with his dad. Then his mum arrived – with two computer games, a real baseball glove and travel chess.

Alex heard Harry's whistle before he saw him. The tune was "Happy Birthday To You!" And he was pushing a trolley piled high with boxes of pizza. Tied to the top was a big red balloon.

"Party time, everyone!" called Harry.

He pulled across some chairs. Children from beds all along the ward came to join in. When it arrived, the birthday cake was big enough for them all to share. Harry put out the lights and everyone sang.

After he'd blown out the candles, Alex looked across at Harry and smiled.

Harry winked. "What did I tell you?" he asked.

"A birthday's a birthday – wherever you are!" laughed Alex.

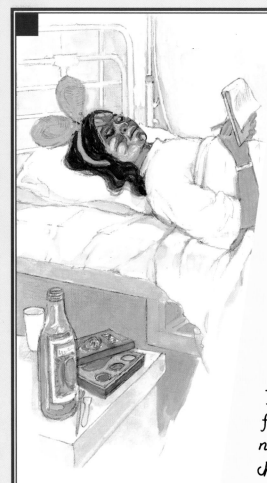

Dear Auntie Jan,

Thanks for coming and bringing me the face paints. We had a laugh with them.

I did what you said and told Mr Green the teacher here about Sammie and Kim. We came up with the idea of making a tape for everyone at school. So I told them all about my operation and what it's like being in hospital. Then I got a card from the whole class and Sammie and Kim and some of the others came to visit me. Mrs Barlow came too. They said they're making a tape for me.

I go back to school after half-term. I'm looking forward to it. But I'll miss everyone here. I'll need to come back in six weeks time to be checked. Louise the playworker says I can come in any time and help in the playroom.

Lots of love

Anya

Dear Anya,

Thank you for your letter and the crazy drawing of yourself! It's great. I've put it on my noticeboard. It must be hard to draw when you are flat on your back.

I'm glad things have worked out so well for you and that you're looking forward to going back to school. After six weeks, you'll probably be really looking forward to going back to hospital for your check up. I expect you will find it strange to be an 'outpatient', just visiting the hospital and not staying.

I'm sure your Mum and Dad will be pleased to have you home. Give them my love.

Lots of love

Auntie Jan

HELPLINES

If you are worried and you feel really alone, you could telephone or write to one of these offices. Sometimes the telephone lines are busy. If they are, don't give up. Try them again.

Action for Sick Children
Telephone 0171 833 2041
(Open Monday - Wednesday 9am-5pm)

ChildLine
Freephone 0800 1111
Address ChildLine Freepost 1111
London N1 0BR

The Samaritans
Telephone 0345 909090